Doughnuts

Simple and Delicious Recipes to Make at Home

Lara Ferroni

SASQUATCH BOOKS
SEATTLE

Printed in the United States of America

Published by Sasquatch Books

15 14 13 12 11 | 9 8 7 6 5 4

Cover photograph: Lara Ferroni

Interior photographs: Lara Ferroni

Interior design and composition: Rosebud Eustace

Library of Congress Cataloging-in-Publication Data

Ferroni, Lara.

    Doughnuts : simple and delicious recipes to make at home / Lara Ferroni.

        p. cm.

    Includes index.

    ISBN-13: 978-1-57061-641-9

    ISBN-10: 1-57061-641-8

    1. Doughnuts. I. Title.

    TX770.D67.F47 2010

    641.8'653—dc22

                                2010003612

Sasquatch Books

1904 Third Avenue, Suite 710

Seattle, WA 98101

(206) 467-4300

www.sasquatchbooks.com

custserv@sasquatchbooks.com

CONTENTS

INTRODUCTION

When I was growing up, doughnuts were the exception, not the rule. They were reserved for one very special time: the road trip. Each summer our family of four would pile into our ridiculously small car and head out across the country to visit an aunt or cousin or grandparent. Trips going west meant little boxes of sugared cereal eaten at a roadside Holiday Inn. But trips northward meant the best thing imaginable to my eight-year-old self: Dunkin' Donuts.

My brother always ordered the chocolate dipped. I would stand on my tip-toes and carefully examine each flavor, imagining how the pastry would feel and taste as I took my first bite. Despite careful deliberation, I always decided between the same two flavors: the Chocolate Kreme Filled and the Dunkin' Donut. The Dunkin' Donut was about as simple as it gets: an old-fashioned cake doughnut with a hint of spice ingeniously shaped with a handle for dipping into a fresh cup of joe. I never actually dunked my doughnut, but I liked the little handle anyway. The Chocolate Kreme Filled was a fluffy raised doughnut filled with almost fluffier milk chocolate frosting and coated with powdered sugar.

While I'll always love those doughnuts, my tastes have also expanded. My husband, who hails from Hamilton, Ontario (the birthplace of Canada's famous doughnut shop, Tim Hortons), turned me on to the ethereal Honey Cruller. Living in Seattle, it's hard to avoid the temptations of Top Pot (Raspberry-Glazed Chocolate Old-Fashioned!) and Mighty O (French Toast!), and all too easy to make a quick drive north of the city to Frost (Bourbon Caramel Pecan!). I've even ventured to Portland just to try Voodoo Doughnut's wonderfully crazy creations, like the Bacon Maple Bar and the Dirt doughnut, and to San Francisco to gorge on Dynamo Donut's eclectic varieties.

Being surrounded by all those glorious pastries made me wonder if maybe, just maybe, I could make doughnuts at home. The notion of a fresh, warm doughnut pushed me past my initial deep-frying anxiety. How glad I am that it did! Making doughnuts is far simpler than I could have imagined, and my fear of hot oil was quickly banished. Before long I was dreaming up flavors for my own sinfully satisfying doughnuts, and I'm delighted to share the best of those recipes here with you. So go ahead, treat yourself. Like me, you'll be happy you did . . . and so will those around you!

DOUGHNUT BASICS

Before you get started with your first batch of dough, I encourage you to read through this section for an overview of doughnut making and general tips and tricks on ingredients and tools.

How This Book Is Organized

The first section of recipes is all about the basics of doughnut making. In it, you'll find recipes for raised and cake doughs, including chocolate doughs, doughs that can be baked instead of fried, and doughs for vegan and gluten-free diets. You'll find many well-known specialty doughs—like old-fashioned sour cream, ricotta, apple cider, and French cruller—as well as some that are less familiar, like *picarones* from Peru and *malasadas* from Portugal. You'll also find recipes for basic glazes that work with these doughs—mix and match to your heart's content.

For something a little more special, turn to the Flavors section, where you'll find even more interesting combinations, from Apple Pie to Crème Brûlée. Each of these recipes refers back to a dough recipe type. Pick the dough that works best for you (traditional, baked, vegan, or gluten-free), then follow the recipe as directed.

If you're planning ahead, it is worth noting that unfilled, unglazed doughnuts can be frozen once they are cooled. To reheat, microwave for 8 to 10 seconds.

A note for those cooking vegan and gluten-free doughnuts: Not all of the variations on the basic recipes include vegan or gluten-free instructions, but most should be easily convertible by using readily available substitutions. Gluten-free

doughnuts can be a bit harder to fill than their wheat-based counterparts because by their very nature they are more dense. To make things a bit easier, use a chopstick to hollow out the middle of the doughnut before using the piping tip.

Ingredients

For best results, all your ingredients (including milk, eggs, yogurt, sour cream, and butter) should be at room temperature when they are used.

FLOUR

Choose your flour based on which type of doughnut you are making. Hard, high-protein flours, such as bread flour, work best for yeast-raised doughnuts. However, if your doughnuts are a bit too tough or heavy, try a blend of bread and unbleached all-purpose flours. Unbleached all-purpose flour is best for cake doughnuts, but if your doughnuts fall flat when removed from the fryer, next time mix in a little bread flour.

Different flour brands have different protein contents and densities, both of which can dramatically affect the consistency of the dough. Even the humidity of the day can change how much flour fills up a measuring cup. It is best to use weight measurements if you can, but if you need to use cup measurements, use the spoon and swipe method on freshly sifted flour. You may still need to adjust the amount of flour in the recipe to achieve the perfect consistency based on your flour brand. I typically use either King Arthur flours or a locally grown and milled flour that measures between 135 and 150 grams per cup.

If you can't eat wheat, I think you'll be quite pleased with the gluten-free raised and cake doughnuts in this book. Doughnuts require a very lightweight gluten-free baking mix that doesn't have a strong flavor. My friend and author Shauna James Ahern helped me develop the following mix, which works well in both the cake and yeast doughnuts, with the use of a binder such as guar or xanthan gum.

Gluten-Free Baking Mix for Doughnuts

Makes enough for a standard doughnut recipe

> 1 cup (175 grams) potato starch
>
> ¼ cup (100 grams) potato flour or sweet sorghum
>
> ½ cup (60 grams) tapioca flour
>
> ½ cup (60 grams) sweet rice flour

LEAVENING

Raised doughnuts use yeast as their primary leavening agent. All the yeast-raised doughnut recipes here call for active dry yeast; if you are using fresh cake yeast, you'll need to double the quantity listed in each recipe. If you think you'll be making yeast-raised doughnuts fairly regularly, it's far more cost-effective to buy active dry yeast in bulk, rather than in individual packages; store this quantity of yeast in the refrigerator.

Baking powder and, for some recipes, baking soda provide leavening for cake doughnuts. Whenever baking powder is called for in a recipe, it's best to use an aluminum-free double-acting baking powder.

Proofing and resting

Yeast doughs have to rest for a while to let the yeast do its business and aerate the dough, which makes the doughnuts soft and light and develops the flavor. The basic yeast (raised) dough recipe in this book has three separate proofing stages. The first is creating a soft "sponge," which jump-starts the yeast into action. The second is a longer rise, done either in a warm environment (70° to 80°F) or in the refrigerator, depending on the recipe. The third and final stage occurs after the dough has been rolled and cut. In this stage, the temperature of the dough and the room can have a big impact on how long it takes to achieve the right amount of rise, so the time needed can vary considerably; keep a close eye on the dough, checking at five-minute intervals. When properly proofed, the doughnut rings will be quite puffy and rounded, but still springy.

Cake doughnuts don't need to proof, but they do need a resting period to give the flour a chance to absorb the liquid. Without this rest, cake doughnuts can take up too much oil from the fryer and become heavy and greasy.

SUGAR

These recipes are best made using superfine sugar, which melts into the dough smoothly and works beautifully to coat the doughnuts after frying with a quick shake in a bag. If you are using regular granulated sugar, which is less dense than superfine, follow the weight measurements or heap your volume measurements.

FATS AND OILS

Fat incorporated into the dough helps prevent the dough from absorbing too much oil while frying, so don't be tempted to skimp. Solid fats like coconut oil, vegetable shortening, lard, or unsalted butter work best. Liquid fats tend to "run out" of the doughnut, leaving a greasy mess once the doughnut has cooled.

For deep-frying, I recommend safflower oil, which is inexpensive and very heat tolerant. Peanut oil is another great choice, if you are cooking for those without nut allergies. Canola oil and sunflower oil are also good choices.

How much oil you need will depend on the size of your pot. You should fill your pot with a depth of at least 2 inches of oil, leaving at least 2 inches from the top of the oil to the top of the pot.

You can use the same frying oil several times, but it is important to strain out any particles between uses and to change the oil completely if it starts to get dark or if your doughnuts are starting to feel too greasy on the surface even when cooked at the right temperature. Old oil leads to greasy, off-tasting doughnuts.

When you are done with your oil, make sure you dispose of it properly according to your city's regulations. Do not pour it down the drain, or you may find yourself quickly racking up plumbing expenses! If you compost, you can stir small amounts of oil in with other organic material. Most cities also have residential cooking oil drop-off locations, where the used oil is recycled into biodiesel. You might also check with local restaurants to see whether you can add your used oil to their grease bins.

And of course, deep-frying should always be done with caution. *Never* leave a pot of oil heating on the stove unattended!

Tools

Doughnut cutters

All you really need is a biscuit cutter (or even an upside-down glass) to make doughnuts, but a doughnut cutter that cuts the holes out at the same time is a nice little gadget to have and should run you only about $6. Make sure you get one that is made from very firm metal and doesn't bend easily as some cookie cutters do.

A large, heavy-bottomed pot

Even though I own a deep fryer, I prefer to use a small Dutch oven to fry dough-nuts. It uses less oil, and cleanup is a bit easier. Just make sure that your pot is deep enough to hold at least 2 inches of oil with at least 2 inches of clearance from the top of the pot.

A fast, accurate thermometer

If you are frying on the stove top, a fast, accurate thermometer that can mea-sure up to 400°F is a must-have. Make sure yours is working properly with this simple test: Bring a pot of water to a boil on the stove. Meanwhile, fill a glass with ice water. Now stick your thermometer in the ice water (you may not be able to get a reading if your thermometer doesn't go that low; that's OK). When the water comes to a boil, move the thermometer to the boiling water, being careful not to touch the tip to the bottom of the pan. Pay attention to how long it takes to come up to boiling (212°F). If it takes more than 30 seconds, consider getting a faster thermometer.

A stand mixer with a dough hook

It's certainly possible to make any dough in this book without a stand mixer and a dough hook, but if you have one, you should use it. You *can* make them by hand—and skip your upper-arm workout at the gym. Using a hand mixer or even mixing by hand with a wooden spoon is fine for any of the cake doughs, but not recommended where a dough hook is specifically called for.

A pastry cloth

I've found that the best material on which to place rising yeast doughnuts—without getting the dough stuck to it—is either linen or a tight-weave, non-terrycloth towel, well dusted with flour. You can also use parchment paper during the proofing stage, but the dough may stick a bit. If it does, try greasing the paper with some cooking spray.

A piping bag and parchment paper

Some doughnuts are lighter and fluffier when made from a batter instead of a shapeable dough. Professional doughnut shops use a special doughnut dropper to make perfect rings that drop directly into the hot oil. Inexpensive versions are also available online, but they don't work as well with the cake recipes in this book as simply piping the batter with a pastry bag onto little squares of greased parchment, and then dropping the doughnut, parchment and all, into the oil. The parchment will slide off easily once the doughnut has started to brown. (For full details on this technique, see the Basic Cake recipe on page 17). If you do want to use a doughnut dropper, you'll need to increase the liquid in the recipes to achieve a pancake-batter consistency.

For filled doughnuts, a needle-like Bismarck (#230) tip works best to inject the filling without creating too much of a hole. A star tip will work in a pinch.

Doughnut pans

If you are baking cake doughnuts, you'll need to buy a special doughnut pan with a rounded cup for each doughnut. Without one, your cake doughnuts will spread and have very flat, hard bottoms. You don't need a special pan for baking raised doughnuts, though. Although the bottoms will be slightly flatter than their fried counterparts, it's barely noticeable.

Doughnut machines

There are all sorts of electric gadgets for making mini doughnuts. You don't need any of them to make doughnuts at home, but they certainly make for some fun party entertainment.

For even more on doughnuts, visit my blog at www.doughnutcookbook.com.

DOUGHS AND GLAZES

DOUGHS

Basic Raised

Baked Raised

Gluten-Free Basic Raised

Vegan Raised

Chocolate Raised

Malasadas

Basic Cake

Baked Cake

Gluten-Free Cake

Vegan Cake

Chocolate Cake

Old-Fashioned Sour Cream

Ricotta

Apple Cider

French Crullers

Sopapillas

Loukoumades

Picarones

GLAZES

Basic Sugar

Chocolate

Honey

Maple

Citrus

Cinnamon Spice

Brown Butter

Bourbon

Caramel

DOUGHS

BASIC RAISED

The quintessential doughnut: fluffy, sweet, heavenly. There's nothing like a still-warm raised doughnut to bring a smile to your face. This basic dough recipe is very subtly sweet, so you can glaze away with your favorite flavors and not worry about the doughnuts getting cloying. *Photo on page xvi.*

Makes 8 to 14 doughnuts
Active time: 20 minutes | Ready in: 2 hours

3 tablespoons (22 grams) active dry yeast, divided

1 cup whole milk, heated to 110°F, divided

2 to 2½ cups (320 to 400 grams) bread flour, divided

2 tablespoons (30 grams) superfine sugar

½ teaspoon salt

1 teaspoon vanilla extract

3 egg yolks

¼ cup (½ stick or 2 ounces) unsalted butter or vegetable shortening

Vegetable oil for frying

1. In a medium bowl, dissolve 2 tablespoons of the yeast into ¾ cup of the milk. Add ¾ cup of the flour and stir to create a smooth paste. Cover and let rest in a warm spot for 30 minutes.

2. Combine the remaining milk and yeast in the bowl of a stand mixer fitted with the paddle attachment. Add the rested flour mixture along with the sugar, salt, vanilla, and egg yolks. Mix until smooth. Turn off the mixer and add ½ cup of the remaining flour. Mix on low for about 30 seconds. Add the butter and mix until it becomes incorporated, about 30 seconds. Switch to a dough hook and add more flour, about ¼ cup at a time with the mixer

turned off, kneading the dough at medium speed between additions, until the dough pulls completely away from the sides of the bowl and is smooth and not too sticky. It will be very soft and moist, but not so sticky that you can't roll it out. You may have flour left over. Cover the bowl with plastic wrap and refrigerate for at least 1 hour (and up to 12 hours).

3. Line a baking sheet with a lightly floured non-terry dish towel. Roll out the dough on a lightly floured surface to ½ inch thick. With a doughnut or cookie cutter, cut out 3-inch-diameter rounds with 1-inch-diameter holes (for filled doughnuts, don't cut out the holes).

4. Place the doughnuts on the baking sheet at least 1 inch apart and cover with plastic wrap. Let sit in a warm spot to proof until they almost double in size, 5 to 20 minutes, testing at five-minute intervals. To test whether the dough is ready, touch lightly with a fingertip. If it springs back immediately, it needs more time. If it springs back slowly, it is ready. If it doesn't spring back at all, it has overproofed; you can punch it down and reroll it once.

5. While the doughnuts are proofing, heat a heavy-bottomed pot with at least 2 inches of oil until a deep-fat thermometer registers 360°F. With a metal spatula, carefully place the doughnuts in the oil. Fry for 1 to 2 minutes per side, or until light golden brown. Remove with a slotted spoon, drain on a wire rack over a paper towel, and let cool slightly before glazing.

BAKED RAISED

Most baked sweet doughs end up more like bagels than doughnuts, but these, based on a Finnish sweet dough recipe, are so soft and light you may not realize they were baked. A quick dip in glaze will keep the crust from becoming too chewy, but they are still best eaten straight away.

Makes 10 to 14 doughnuts
Active time: 20 minutes | Ready in: 2 hours

> 1 egg
>
> ¼ cup (60 grams) superfine sugar
>
> 1 cup whole milk, heated to 115°F
>
> 1 tablespoon (8 grams) active dry yeast
>
> 1 teaspoon salt
>
> 2 teaspoons vanilla extract
>
> 2½ to 3½ cups (300 to 420 grams) all-purpose flour, divided, plus more
>   for kneading
>
> ½ cup (1 stick or 4 ounces) butter, cut into 1-inch cubes

1. In the bowl of a stand mixer fitted with the paddle attachment, beat the egg and sugar on medium speed until blended, about 1 minute. Add the milk, yeast, salt, and vanilla, and stir to blend. With the machine on low speed, add 2 cups of flour, about ½ cup at a time, and beat until the dough is thick and pulls away from the sides of the bowl.

2. Switch to the dough hook. With the machine on medium speed, add the butter one piece at a time, and beat until no large chunks of butter are left in the bottom of the bowl, 3 to 5 minutes. Reduce speed to low and add additional flour until the dough gathers around the hook and cleans the sides of the bowl. It will be soft and moist, but not overly sticky.

3. Turn the dough out onto a floured surface and knead gently until the dough no longer sticks to your hands. Lightly grease a large mixing bowl.

Transfer the dough to the bowl and turn to coat. Cover with a damp tea towel and let rise in a warm spot until doubled in volume, about 1 hour.

4. Punch down the dough and roll out to ½ inch thick. With a doughnut or cookie cutter, cut out 3-inch-diameter rounds with 1-inch-diameter holes (for filled doughnuts, don't cut out the holes).

5. Preheat the oven to 400°F and line a baking sheet with parchment paper. Place the doughnuts at least 1 inch apart on the baking sheet. Cover with plastic wrap and let sit in a warm spot until nearly doubled in size, about 20 minutes.

6. Bake until the doughnuts are a light golden brown, 5 to 8 minutes, being very careful not to overbake them. Immediately brush with butter and sugar or glaze, and eat while still warm.

GLUTEN-FREE BASIC RAISED

If you can find it, chia flour (yep, the same seeds used on the Chia Pet!) helps add just the right amount of chew to help these gluten-free raised doughnuts mimic their traditional counterparts.

Makes 8 to 14 doughnuts
Active time: 20 minutes | Ready in: 1 hour 45 minutes

⅓ cup (50 grams) chia flour or brown rice flour

1½ to 2 cups (215 to 290 grams) Gluten-Free Baking Mix for Doughnuts (page x)

¼ teaspoon xanthan gum

¼ teaspoon guar gum

1½ teaspoons baking powder

1½ tablespoons (11 grams) active dry yeast, divided

¼ cup whole milk, heated to 110°F

¼ cup lukewarm water

3 tablespoons (45 grams) superfine sugar

½ teaspoon salt

2 large eggs

1 large egg white

1 teaspoon vanilla extract

1 teaspoon apple cider vinegar

2 tablespoons (1 ounce) unsalted butter or vegetable shortening

Vegetable oil for frying

1. Whisk together the flour, gluten-free baking mix, xanthan gum, guar gum, and baking powder and set aside.

2. In a medium bowl, dissolve 1 tablespoon of the yeast in the milk. Add ⅛ cup (20 grams) of the flour mixture and stir to create a thick paste. Cover and let rest in a warm spot for 15 minutes.

3. In the bowl of a stand mixer fitted with the paddle attachment, stir together the remaining yeast and the lukewarm water. Add the flour paste mixture along with the sugar and salt. Mix until smooth. Beat in the eggs, egg white, vanilla, and vinegar. Turn off the mixer and add ½ cup of the reserved flour mixture. Mix in completely and knead on medium speed for about 30 seconds. Add the butter and mix to combine. Switch to the dough hook, and add the remaining flour mixture, about ¼ cup at a time with the mixer turned off, kneading the dough at medium speed between additions, until the dough just starts to pull away from the sides of the bowl and gets raggedy. It will be very soft and moist, but not so sticky that you can't roll it out. You may have flour left over.

4. Place the dough in a large resealable bag (or cover the bowl with plastic wrap) and let rest in a warm spot for 20 minutes. Roll out the dough on a lightly floured surface to ½ inch thick. With a doughnut or cookie cutter, cut out 3-inch-diameter rounds with 1-inch-diameter holes (for filled doughnuts, don't cut out the holes).

5. Line a baking sheet with a lightly floured non-terry dish towel. Place the doughnuts at least 1 inch apart and cover with plastic wrap. Let sit in a warm spot until they are nicely rounded on top, 20 to 30 minutes.

6. While the doughnuts are proofing, heat a heavy-bottomed pot with at least 2 inches of oil until a deep-fat thermometer registers 340°F. With a metal spatula, carefully place the doughnuts in the oil. Don't overfill the pot. Fry for 1 to 2 minutes per side, or until light golden brown. Remove with a slotted spoon. Place on a wire rack and let cool slightly before glazing or filling.

VEGAN RAISED

No animal products are required in this super light and fluffy raised dough.

Makes 8 to 14 doughnuts
Active time: 20 minutes | Ready in: 2 hours

> 3 tablespoons (22 grams) active dry yeast, divided
>
> 1 cup soy milk, heated to 110°F, divided
>
> 2 to 2½ cups (320 to 400 grams) bread flour, divided
>
> 2 tablespoons (30 grams) superfine sugar
>
> ½ teaspoon salt
>
> 1 teaspoon vanilla extract
>
> 2 tablespoons potato starch
>
> 4 tablespoons (2 ounces) vegetable shortening, melted
>
> Vegetable oil for frying

1. In a medium bowl, dissolve 2 tablespoons of the yeast in ¾ cup of the milk. Add ¾ cup of the flour and stir to create a smooth paste. Cover and let rest in a warm spot for 30 minutes.

2. In the bowl of a stand mixer fitted with the paddle attachment, stir together the remaining milk and yeast. Add the yeast paste along with the sugar, salt, vanilla, and potato starch. Mix until smooth. Turn off the mixer and add ½ cup of the remaining flour. Mix on low for about 30 seconds. Add the shortening and mix until it becomes incorporated, about 30 seconds. Switch to a dough hook. Add more flour as directed for Basic Raised doughnuts on page 2.

3. Cover the bowl with plastic wrap and refrigerate for at least 1 hour (and up to 12 hours). Roll and cut the doughnuts, let rise, and fry as directed for Basic Raised doughnuts on page 2.

CHOCOLATE RAISED

Most chocolate doughnuts in bakeries are cake doughnuts. But for the true chocoholic, try this raised dough, which brings a fun chocolaty twist to basic raised doughnuts. Use Dutch processed cocoa powder for the most chocolaty flavor.

Makes 6 to 12 doughnuts
Active time: 20 minutes | Ready in: 2 hours

> 3 tablespoons (22 grams) active dry yeast
>
> 1 cup whole milk, heated to 110°F
>
> 2 to 2½ cups (320 to 400 grams) bread flour, divided
>
> ¼ cup (60 grams) superfine sugar
>
> ½ teaspoon salt
>
> ½ teaspoon baking soda
>
> 1 teaspoon vanilla extract
>
> 3 egg yolks
>
> ⅓ cup (28 grams) Dutch processed cocoa powder
>
> 4 tablespoons (2 ounces) unsalted butter or vegetable shortening
>
> Vegetable oil for frying

1. In a medium bowl, dissolve 2 tablespoons of the yeast into ¾ cup of the warm milk. Add ¾ cup of the flour and stir to create a smooth paste. Cover and let rest in a warm spot for 30 minutes.

2. Stir together the remaining warm milk and yeast in the bowl of a stand mixer fitted with the paddle attachment. Add the rested flour mixture along with the sugar, salt, baking soda, vanilla, and egg yolks. Mix until smooth. Stir in the cocoa powder. Turn off the mixer and add ½ cup of the remaining flour. Mix on low for about 30 seconds. Add the butter and mix for about 30 seconds or until it becomes incorporated. Add the remaining flour as directed for Basic Raised doughnuts on page 2.

3. Cover the bowl with plastic wrap and refrigerate for at least 1 hour (and up to 12 hours). Roll and cut the doughnuts, let rise, and fry as directed for Basic Raised doughnuts on page 2.

MALASADAS

Malasadas are a yeast doughnut that originated in Portugal and became very popular in Hawaii, where they are served hot, dusted with sugar or filled with custard or fruit preserves.

Makes 24 to 36 malasadas
Active time: 30 minutes | Ready in: 3 hours

2 tablespoons lukewarm water

1 tablespoon (11 grams) yeast

½ cup (120 grams) superfine sugar, divided, plus additional for dusting

3 large eggs

2 tablespoons (1 ounce) unsalted butter or vegetable shortening, melted

½ cup whole milk

½ cup half-and-half

¼ teaspoon salt

3 to 4 cups (480 to 640 grams) bread flour

Vegetable oil for frying

1. Place the water in a small bowl and sprinkle with the yeast and 1 teaspoon of the sugar. Stir and set aside until foamy, about 5 minutes.

2. In the bowl of a stand mixer fitted with the paddle attachment, beat the eggs until thick. Add the yeast mixture, butter, remaining sugar, milk, half-and-half, and salt. Mix until just combined.

3. Switch to the dough hook attachment and add the flour ½ cup at a time, until the mixture forms a soft dough that pulls away from the edges of the bowl. The dough will be moist, but not too sticky.

4. Cover the dough with plastic wrap and let it rise in a warm spot until it doubles in volume, about 1 hour. Flip the dough over, cover, and let rise for another hour until it doubles again.

5. Heat a heavy-bottomed pot with at least 2 inches of oil until a deep-fat thermometer registers 350°F.

6. On a lightly floured surface, roll the dough to ½ inch thick, then with a knife cut it into 1-inch squares. For more rustic-looking malasadas, you can just pinch off small balls of the dough and press them flat between your palms.

7. With a metal spatula, carefully place in the oil. Fry until golden, 1 to 2 minutes on each side. Remove from the oil with a slotted spoon. Drain briefly on a paper towel. Shake in a brown bag filled with superfine sugar. Serve immediately.

BASIC CAKE

Making these subtly spiced cake doughnuts is so easy and quick. They are the perfect pairing with coffee, in the morning or even for dessert.

Makes 6 to 10 traditional doughnuts or 25 to 35 drop doughnuts
Active time: 15 minutes | Ready in: 40 minutes

1¾ cups (240 grams) all-purpose flour, sifted

2 teaspoons baking powder

½ teaspoon salt

1 teaspoon freshly grated nutmeg

⅓ cup (75 grams) superfine sugar

2 tablespoons (1 ounce) unsalted butter or vegetable shortening

1 egg

½ cup whole milk, scalded and divided

2 tablespoons plain yogurt

1 teaspoon vanilla extract

Vegetable oil for frying

1. In the bowl of a stand mixer fitted with the paddle attachment, combine the flour, baking powder, salt, nutmeg, and sugar. Blend on low speed. Add the butter and blend at medium-low speed. The mixture should resemble coarse sand.

2. In a separate bowl, combine the egg, ¼ cup of the milk, yogurt, and vanilla. With the mixer running, slowly pour the wet ingredients into the flour-butter mixture. Scrape down the sides of the bowl and mix for 20 seconds. Mix in the remaining milk, a little at a time, until the batter sticks to the sides of the bowl. The batter should be smooth, thick, and spoonable, similar to moist cookie dough. You may not need all of the milk. Cover with plastic wrap and let rest for 15 to 20 minutes.

3. Heat at least 2 inches of oil in a heavy-bottomed pot until a deep-fat thermometer registers 360°F.

4. For traditional doughnuts, fill a piping bag fitted with a ⅓-inch round tip. Calculate how many 3-inch doughnuts can fry in your pot at one time. Grease a 4-by-4-inch parchment square for each and pipe a 3-inch-diameter ring onto each square. Carefully place one in the oil, parchment side up. Remove the parchment with tongs and repeat with a few more rings, being careful not to overfill the pan. Cook for 1 to 2 minutes on each side, or until light golden brown. For drop doughnuts, just drop tablespoon-size dollops directly into the oil and fry for about 45 seconds per side, or until light golden brown.

5. Remove with a slotted spoon and drain on a paper towel. Repeat with the remaining batter. Let cool just slightly before glazing and eating.

BAKED CAKE

Cake doughnuts are fried, not baked, at your local doughnut shop. But this recipe bakes up just as delicious, and cleanup is far easier, not to mention a bit less guilt-inducing. This batter also bakes up beautifully in an electric doughnut maker.

Note: To get the proper doughnut shape when baking cake doughnuts, you do need a doughnut pan with a rounded bottom to each cup and a post through the middle. Baking them on a flat baking sheet will result in flat-bottomed half-doughnuts. If you don't have a doughnut pan, you can make the same batter and bake it in a muffin tin for doughnut-flavored muffins. The batter also works great with a mini-muffin pan for bite-size treats.

Makes 6 to 12 doughnuts
Prep time: 15 minutes | Ready in: 30 minutes

¾ cup plus 1 tablespoon (120 grams) all-purpose flour

¼ cup (30 grams) whole wheat pastry flour

1 teaspoon baking powder

⅓ cup (75 grams) superfine sugar

½ teaspoon freshly grated nutmeg

½ teaspoon salt

2 tablespoons (1 ounce) unsalted butter or vegetable shortening

¼ cup whole milk, scalded

¼ cup plain yogurt

1 teaspoon vanilla extract

1 egg, beaten

1. Preheat the oven to 350°F. Lightly grease a doughnut pan.

2. Sift the flours and baking powder together into a large bowl or the bowl of a mixer. Whisk in the sugar, nutmeg, and salt. Add the butter and use your

fingers to rub it into the dry ingredients as you would in making a pastry crust, until evenly distributed. Add the milk, yogurt, vanilla, and egg and stir until just combined. Do not overmix or your doughnuts may be rubbery.

3. Use a piping bag or a spoon to fill each doughnut cup about three-quarters full, making sure the center post is clear. Bake until doughnuts are a light golden brown and spring back when touched, 6 to 10 minutes. Let cool slightly before removing from pan. Glaze as desired.

GLUTEN-FREE CAKE

These lightly spiced cake doughnuts are a real treat for those who can't tolerate gluten in their diet.

Makes 8 to 10 traditional doughnuts or 25 to 35 drop doughnuts
Active time: 15 minutes | Ready in: 40 minutes

2 cups (280 grams) Gluten-Free Baking Mix for Doughnuts (page x)

½ teaspoon guar gum

1 tablespoon baking powder

½ teaspoon salt

2 teaspoons freshly grated nutmeg

⅓ cup (75 grams) superfine sugar

¼ cup (½ stick or 2 ounces) unsalted butter or vegetable shortening

2 eggs, separated

¼ cup plain yogurt

⅔ cup whole milk, scalded and cooled

2 teaspoons vanilla extract

Pinch of cream of tartar

Vegetable oil for frying

1. In the bowl of a stand mixer fitted with the paddle attachment, combine the gluten-free baking mix, guar gum, baking powder, salt, nutmeg, and sugar. Blend on low. Add the butter and blend on medium-low. The mixture should resemble coarse sand.

2. In a separate bowl, combine the egg yolks, yogurt, milk, and vanilla. With the mixer running, slowly pour the wet ingredients into the flour mixture. Scrape down the sides and mix for 30 seconds. The batter should be smooth, thick, and spoonable, similar to loose cookie dough. Let rest for 15 to 20 minutes.

3. Heat at least 2 inches of oil in a heavy-bottomed pot until a deep-fat thermometer registers 350°F.

4. Whisk the egg whites and cream of tartar until soft peaks form. Fold into the rested batter. Pipe the batter and fry as directed for Basic Cake doughnuts on page 17.

Variation: For a chocolate version, add ¼ cup (15 grams) natural cocoa powder, ½ teaspoon baking soda, and an additional 2 tablespoons superfine sugar into the flour mixture.

VEGAN CAKE

Most vegan cake doughnut recipes are baked instead of fried, mostly to make them a bit healthier, but also because without eggs, the dough doesn't hold together well when fried. Adding a bit of guar gum helps bind the dough for fully formed rings.

Makes 6 to 10 traditional doughnuts or 25 to 35 drop doughnuts
Active time: 15 minutes | Ready in: 40 minutes

1¼ cups (160 grams) all-purpose flour

1 teaspoon baking powder

¼ teaspoon guar gum

⅓ cup (75 grams) superfine sugar

1 teaspoon freshly grated nutmeg

½ teaspoon salt

2 tablespoons (1 ounce) vegetable shortening

½ cup plain almond or soy milk, divided

2 tablespoons plain soy yogurt

½ teaspoon vinegar

½ teaspoon vanilla

Vegetable oil for frying

1. Combine the flour, baking powder, guar gum, sugar, nutmeg, and salt in the bowl of a stand mixer fitted with the paddle attachment. Turn mixer on low to blend all the dry ingredients together. Add the shortening, turn the mixer up to medium-low, and blend. The mixture should resemble coarse sand.

2. In a separate bowl, mix ¼ cup almond milk, soy yogurt, vinegar, and vanilla together. With the mixer running, slowly pour the wet ingredients into the flour mixture. Scrape down the sides of the bowl and mix for 20 seconds. Mix in the remaining almond milk, a little at a time, until the batter sticks to the sides of the bowl. The batter should be smooth, thick, and spoonable,

similar to loose cookie dough. You may not need to use all of your almond milk. Cover the dough with plastic wrap and let rest for 15 to 20 minutes.

3. Heat at least 2 inches of oil in a heavy-bottomed pot until a deep-fat thermometer registers 360°F.

4. For traditional doughnuts, fill a piping bag fitted with a ⅓-inch round tip. Calculate how many 3-inch doughnuts can fry in your pot at one time. Grease a 4-by-4-inch parchment square for each and pipe a 3-inch-diameter ring onto each square. Carefully place one in the oil, parchment side up. Remove the parchment with tongs, and repeat with a few more rings, being careful not to overfill the pan. Cook for 1 to 2 minutes on each side, or until light golden brown. For drop doughnuts, just drop tablespoon-size dollops directly into the oil and fry for about 45 seconds per side, or until light golden brown.

5. Remove with a slotted spoon and drain on a paper towel. Repeat with the remaining batter. Let cool just slightly before glazing and eating.

Variation: For a chocolate version, add ¼ cup (15 grams) natural cocoa powder, ½ teaspoon baking soda, and an additional 2 tablespoons superfine sugar into the flour mixture.

CHOCOLATE CAKE

These rich chocolate cake doughnuts are a bit more chocolaty than the dough-nuts you find in chain doughnut stores, which, let's face it, are more *brown* than chocolate. If you prefer them less chocolaty, you can reduce the amount of cocoa powder to ¼ cup. If you use Dutch processed cocoa powder, use half the amount of baking soda.

Makes 6 to 10 doughnuts
Active time: 15 minutes | Ready in: 40 minutes

> 1¾ cups (240 grams) all-purpose flour, sifted
>
> ⅓ cup (27 grams) unsweetened natural cocoa powder
>
> 1½ teaspoons baking powder
>
> ½ teaspoon baking soda
>
> ½ teaspoon salt
>
> ½ cup (120 grams) superfine sugar
>
> 2 tablespoons butter
>
> 1 egg
>
> ½ cup whole milk, scalded
>
> 1 teaspoon vanilla extract
>
> Vegetable oil for frying

1. Combine the flour, cocoa powder, baking powder, baking soda, salt, and sugar in the bowl of a stand mixer fitted with the paddle attachment. Turn mixer on low to blend all the dry ingredients together. Add the butter and turn the mixer up to medium-low to blend the butter into the dry ingredients. The mix should resemble coarse sand.

2. Stir the egg, milk, and vanilla together in a separate bowl. Pour the wet ingredients into the flour mixture slowly with the mixer running. Scrape down the sides of the bowl and mix for 30 seconds. The batter should be

smooth, thick, and not too wet, similar to sugar cookie dough. Let the dough rest for 15 to 20 minutes

3. Heat at least 2 inches of oil in a heavy-bottomed pot until a deep-fat thermometer registers 360°F.

4. Roll out the dough on a lightly floured surface to ½ inch thick. With a doughnut or cookie cutter, cut out 3-inch-diameter rings with 1-inch-diameter holes.

5. With a metal spatula, carefully place the doughnuts in the oil. Fry for 1 to 2 minutes per side, or until light golden brown. Remove with a slotted spoon and drain on a paper towel. Let cool just slightly before glazing.

OLD-FASHIONED SOUR CREAM

What's the difference between a cake doughnut and an old-fashioned? The two are sibling pastries. Cake doughnuts are the straitlaced ones; old-fashioned, contrary to the name, are a bit on the wild side. As they fry, they split and crack all over the place, making a crisp crust with all sorts of crags to catch glaze and frosting flavors.

Makes 6 to 10 doughnuts
Active time: 15 minutes | Ready in: 40 minutes

> 1 ¼ cups (160 grams) all-purpose flour
>
> 1 teaspoon baking soda
>
> 1 teaspoon cinnamon
>
> Pinch of salt
>
> ⅓ cup (75 grams) superfine sugar
>
> ¼ cup sour cream
>
> 1 large egg
>
> 1 tablespoon (½ ounce) unsalted butter or vegetable shortening
>
> Vegetable oil for frying

1. Sift together the flour, baking soda, and cinnamon. Stir in the salt. Set aside.

2. In a separate medium bowl, whisk together the sugar, sour cream, egg, and butter until smooth. Add the flour mixture a little at a time until a smooth dough forms. Cover the bowl with plastic wrap and refrigerate the batter for 15 to 20 minutes.

3. Roll out the dough on a lightly floured surface to about ½ inch thick, then cut out the doughnuts using a 2½-inch-diameter cutter. You can reroll any scrap dough.

4. Fry as directed for Chocolate Cake doughnuts on page 28.

RICOTTA

This quick and easy batter yields plenty of the fluffiest fritters you've ever tasted.

Makes 10 to 14 traditional doughnuts or 25 to 35 drop doughnuts
Active time: 20 minutes | Ready in: 20 minutes

1 ¼ cups (180 grams) all-purpose flour

2 teaspoons baking powder

¼ cup (60 grams) superfine sugar

1 tablespoon freshly grated lemon zest

3 eggs

8 ounces ricotta cheese

1 teaspoon vanilla extract

Vegetable oil for frying

Confectioners' sugar

Honey glaze (page 48)

1. Sift the flour and baking powder into a medium bowl. Stir in the sugar, lemon zest, eggs, ricotta, and vanilla, mixing just enough to combine. Do not overmix. The batter can be used immediately or stored up to 1 day covered in the refrigerator.

2. Fry as directed for Basic Cake doughnuts on page 17.

3. Sprinkle with confectioners' sugar or drizzle with honey glaze.

APPLE CIDER

A little bit of graham flour makes these doughnuts a bit nuttier and helps them fry up with a wonderfully crisp, nubby crust. However, feel free to replace the graham flour with all-purpose for a more traditional apple cider doughnut.

Makes 10 to 14 doughnuts
Active time: 15 minutes | Ready in: 40 minutes

1¾ cups (240 grams) all-purpose flour

¼ cup (30 grams) graham flour

2 teaspoons cinnamon

2 teaspoons baking powder

1 teaspoon baking soda

½ teaspoon salt

2 tablespoons (1 ounce) unsalted butter or vegetable shortening

½ cup (120 grams) superfine sugar

2 egg yolks

1 teaspoon vanilla extract

¼ cup apple cider

¼ cup buttermilk

Vegetable oil for frying

1. Whisk together the flours, cinnamon, baking powder, baking soda, and salt and set aside.

2. In the bowl of a stand mixer fitted with the paddle attachment, cream the butter and sugar together. Add the egg yolks and beat until the mixture is fluffy and pale yellow. Using a wooden spoon, stir in the vanilla, cider, and buttermilk. Add the dry ingredients and stir just until the mixture comes together to create a soft, slightly sticky dough. Cover and refrigerate for 15 to 20 minutes.

3. Roll out the dough on a lightly floured surface to about ½ inch thick, then cut out the doughnuts using a 2½-inch-diameter cutter. You can reroll any scrap dough.

4. Heat at least 2 inches of oil in a heavy-bottomed pot until a deep-fat thermometer registers 360°F. With a metal spatula, carefully place the doughnuts in the oil. Fry in small batches, being careful not to overcrowd the pot. Cook until a rich golden brown, about 1 minute on each side. Remove with a slotted spoon and drain on a paper towel. Let cool to the touch before glazing and eating.

5. You can also bake these doughnuts in a doughnut pan (in a 350°F oven for 5 to 10 minutes), but you won't achieve the same rich golden color.

FRENCH CRULLERS

There are two kinds of crullers: hand-twisted cake doughnuts, which are more akin to maple bars; and French crullers made with pâte à choux, which are lighter than air, with all sorts of nooks and crannies to hold onto their light honey glaze. These crullers, one of my family's favorites, are the latter.

Note: Undercooked crullers will collapse while cooling, so observe the first one and if this happens, increase your frying time (and check your oil temperature) for the rest.

Makes 10 to 14 crullers
Active time: 30 minutes | Ready in: 30 minutes

> 1 cup water
>
> 6 tablespoons (3 ounces) unsalted butter
>
> 2 teaspoons (10 grams) superfine sugar
>
> ¼ teaspoon salt
>
> 1 cup (135 grams) all-purpose flour, sifted
>
> 3 large eggs, divided
>
> 1 to 2 egg whites, slightly beaten
>
> Vegetable oil for frying
>
> Honey glaze (see page 48)

1. Place the water, butter, sugar, and salt in a heavy-bottomed pot and bring to a brisk boil over medium high heat. Add the flour and stir with a wooden spoon until the flour is completely incorporated. Continue to cook and stir for 3 to 4 minutes to steam away as much water as possible. The more moisture you can remove, the more eggs you can add later and the lighter your pastry will be. The mixture is ready when a thin film coats the bottom of the pan.

2. Move the mixture to the bowl of a stand mixer fitted with the paddle attachment. Although you can mix the pâte à choux by hand, this can be

rather arduous, so use a mixer if you have one. Stir the mixture for about 1 minute to allow it to cool. Then mix on medium speed and add the first egg. Let it mix in completely and then scrape down the sides of the bowl. Add the remaining eggs, one at a time, and mix in completely. Add the egg whites, a little at a time, until the paste becomes smooth and glossy and will hold a slight peak when pinched with your fingers. Be careful not to add too much egg white or your crullers will become heavy. Transfer the batter to a pastry bag fitted with a ½-inch star piping tip.

3. To fry the crullers, heat at least 2 inches of oil in a heavy-bottomed pot until a deep-fat thermometer registers 370°F. While the oil is heating, cut out twelve 3-by-3-inch squares of parchment paper and lightly grease them. Pipe a ring onto each square. When the oil is hot, place one cruller at a time in the oil, paper side up. Remove the paper with tongs. Fry on each side until golden brown, 2 to 3 minutes. Remove with a slotted spoon and drain on a paper towel for at least 1 minute. Once cool to the touch, the crullers can be glazed.

Crullers also bake very well, although they will have slightly firmer crusts than the fried versions. Preheat the oven to 450°F. Line a baking sheet with parchment paper and pipe the crullers onto it, at least 2 inches apart. Bake for 5 minutes, then reduce heat to 350°F and bake for another 15 minutes. Turn off the heat, open the oven door slightly and let the crullers sit in the cooling oven for 5 to 10 minutes. Remove, dip in glaze, and cool on a rack until the glaze has set.

Beignets, the classic New Orleans fried dough treats, use this same batter and are even easier to prepare. Simply drop rounded teaspoonfuls of the batter into the oil. As the dough puffs, the beignets will turn themselves over—but keep an eye on them and flip any that need a little help.

SOPAPILLAS

Unlike the crisp, cinnamon-sugar-and-whipped-cream-covered triangles you find in many Tex-Mex restaurants, these New Mexico–style *sopapillas* are like little pillows of dough and air. Serve a basket of them in place of tortillas alongside a big bowl of chile verde; offer again for dessert with a drizzle of honey.

Makes 6 to 12 sopapillas
Active time: 20 minutes | Ready in: 40 minutes

> 2¼ cups (300 grams) all-purpose flour
>
> 1 teaspoon baking powder
>
> 1 teaspoon salt
>
> 2 tablespoons (1 ounce) shortening or lard
>
> ⅔ cup warm water
>
> Vegetable oil for frying

1. Sift the flour, baking powder, and salt into a medium bowl. Add the shortening and gently work in with your fingertips until the mixture resembles coarse crumbs. Add the water, a little at a time. Mix with a fork until the dough forms a ball. Turn out onto a lightly floured surface and knead for about 30 seconds. Cover and let rest for 30 minutes.

2. Heat at least 2 inches of oil in a heavy-bottomed pot until a deep-fat thermometer registers 370°F.

3. On a lightly floured surface, roll out the dough very thin, ⅛ to ¼ inch thick. Cut into 3-inch squares or triangles.

4. Carefully place in the oil and fry until golden and puffed, 1 to 2 minutes per side. Remove with a slotted spoon and drain on a paper towel, allowing to cool just slightly.

5. Sopapillas are best eaten immediately, but can be kept warm in a 200°F oven for up to 1 hour.

LOUKOUMADES

I first learned of these puffy little fritters, a traditional treat on the island of Cyprus, in Tessa Kiro's beautiful *Falling Cloudberries* cookbook. The honey syrup is amazing, too.

Makes 20 to 30 loukoumades
Active time: 30 minutes | Ready in: 3 hours

½ tablespoon (5 grams) active dry yeast

¾ cup lukewarm water

¾ cup (100 grams) all-purpose flour, divided

Pinch of superfine sugar

Pinch of salt

1 large (about ½ pound) baking potato, peeled and cut in half

¼ cup honey

2 tablespoons freshly squeezed lemon juice

¼ teaspoon ground cinnamon

Vegetable oil for frying

1. In the bowl of a stand mixer, add the yeast to the water. Stir to distribute the yeast. Add ¼ cup of the flour, along with the sugar and salt. Stir again, cover, and let sit for 20 minutes in a warm place.

2. Boil the potato until easily pierced with a fork. Drain, let cool, and mash well.

3. Add the potato and the remaining flour to the yeast mixture. With the paddle attachment or dough hook, beat to form a smooth, wet dough. Cover the bowl and let sit until the batter has thickened, about 2 hours.

4. Meanwhile, make the syrup in a heavy-bottomed pot by stirring together the honey, lemon juice, and cinnamon with a splash of water. Boil on medium-low heat until the mixture thickens, about 10 minutes. Set aside.

5. Heat at least 2 inches of oil in a heavy-bottomed pot until a deep-fat thermometer registers 360°F. Drop in heaping teaspoon–size dollops and fry, turning occasionally, until they are golden and puffed, about 1 minute. Drain on a paper towel and let cool slightly.

6. To serve, place the puffs in a bowl and drizzle with the syrup.

PICARONES

Picarones are sweet, ring-shaped winter squash fritters enjoyed in Peru. Traditionally they are sweetened with *miel de chancaca* (chancaca honey), a sweet sauce made of raw cane sugar and honey flavored with orange. A good sour/sweet marmalade is a simpler and equally delicious substitute.

Makes 6 to 12 picarones
Active time: 30 minutes | Ready in: 2 hours

½ stick cinnamon

4 cloves

2 tablespoons aniseed

1 medium yam, peeled and sliced in half

4 ounces pumpkin or winter squash, peeled and cut into 3-inch chunks

2 teaspoons (6 grams) active dry yeast

1 teaspoon (5 grams) superfine sugar

Pinch of salt

1¼ cups (160 grams) all-purpose flour

Vegetable oil for frying

1. Bring a large pot of water to a boil. Add the cinnamon, cloves, and aniseed and simmer for 10 minutes. Remove the spices and discard them. Add the yam and pumpkin to the water and cook until soft, about 10 minutes.

2. Reserve 2 tablespoons of the cooking water and let cool to about 110°F. Add the yeast and sugar and let sit for 5 minutes.

3. In the bowl of a stand mixer fitted with the paddle attachment, strain the yam and pumpkin and mash to a smooth puree. Stir in the salt and the yeast mixture. Beat until smooth. Add the flour, a little at a time, until a soft, elastic dough forms. If the dough is still sticky, add a bit more flour.

4. Cover the dough and proof in a warm place until doubled in volume, about 1 hour.

5. Heat at least 2 inches of oil in a heavy-bottomed pot until a deep-fat thermometer registers 360°F. Pinch off golf ball–size pieces of dough and shape into rings with your fingers. With a metal spatula, carefully place the rings in the oil and fry on each side until golden. Remove with a slotted spoon, drain on a paper towel, and let cool slightly before serving with the *miel de chancaca* or marmalade on the side.

GLAZES

BASIC SUGAR

Makes enough for a standard doughnut recipe

> 1½ cups (150 grams) confectioners' sugar, sifted to remove any lumps
>
> 3 to 4 tablespoons milk or water
>
> 2 teaspoons vanilla extract (optional)

1. Place the sugar in a medium bowl and slowly stir in the milk and vanilla, a little at a time, to make a smooth, pourable glaze.

CHOCOLATE

Makes enough for a standard doughnut recipe

> 1½ cups (150 grams) confectioners' sugar
>
> 4 tablespoons (27 grams) cocoa powder
>
> 2 tablespoons milk or water
>
> 2 teaspoons vanilla

1. Sift together the sugar and cocoa powder in a medium bowl. Slowly stir in the milk and vanilla, a little at a time, to make a smooth, pourable glaze.

HONEY

Makes enough for a standard doughnut recipe

> 1 ½ cups (150 grams) confectioners' sugar, sifted to remove any lumps
>
> 1 tablespoon honey
>
> 3 to 4 tablespoons milk or water

1. Place the sugar in a medium bowl and slowly stir in the honey and milk, a little at a time, to make a smooth, pourable glaze.

MAPLE

Makes enough for a standard doughnut recipe

> 1 ½ cups (150 grams) confectioners' sugar, sifted to remove any lumps
>
> 2 tablespoons maple syrup
>
> 2 tablespoons milk or water

1. Place the sugar in a medium bowl and slowly stir in the maple syrup and milk, a little at a time, to make a smooth, pourable glaze.

CITRUS

Makes enough for a standard doughnut recipe

> 1 ½ cups (150 grams) confectioners' sugar, sifted to remove any lumps
>
> 3 to 4 tablespoons freshly squeezed citrus juice

1. Place the sugar in a medium bowl and slowly stir in the citrus juice, a little at a time, to make a smooth, pourable glaze.

CINNAMON SPICE

Makes enough for a standard doughnut recipe

> 1½ cups (150 grams) confectioners' sugar, sifted to remove any lumps
>
> ½ teaspoon cinnamon
>
> ½ teaspoon allspice
>
> 3 to 4 tablespoons milk or water

1. Place the sugar in a medium bowl and whisk in the cinnamon and allspice. Slowly stir in the milk, a little at a time, to make a smooth, pourable glaze.

BROWN BUTTER

Makes enough for a standard doughnut recipe

> 3 tablespoons butter
>
> 1½ cups (150 grams) confectioners' sugar, sifted to remove any lumps
>
> 1 to 2 tablespoons milk or water

1. Place the butter in a heavy-bottomed pan and cook over medium heat until the solids in the butter separate and begin to brown. Remove from the heat immediately.

2. Place the sugar in a medium bowl and slowly stir in the brown butter and milk, a little at a time, to make a smooth, pourable glaze. This glaze will quickly firm up, so use it while it is still warm.

BOURBON

Makes enough for a standard doughnut recipe

> 1½ cups (150 grams) confectioners' sugar, sifted to remove any lumps
>
> 2 to 3 tablespoons top-shelf bourbon
>
> 2 teaspoons vanilla extract

1. Place the sugar in a medium bowl and slowly stir in the bourbon and vanilla, a little at a time, to make a smooth, pourable glaze.

CARAMEL

Makes enough for a standard doughnut recipe

> 2½ tablespoons unsalted butter
>
> ¼ cup brown sugar
>
> ¼ cup (60 grams) superfine sugar
>
> ¼ teaspoon sea salt
>
> ¼ cup whole milk
>
> ½ cup (50 grams) confectioners' sugar
>
> 1 teaspoon vanilla extract (optional)

1. Combine the butter, sugars, salt, and milk in a heavy-bottomed pot and cook over medium heat for 3 minutes, stirring occasionally. Remove from heat and let cool.

2. Place the cooled caramel in the bowl of a stand mixer and sift in the confectioners' sugar. Beat until incorporated. Add the vanilla and beat until smooth.

FLAVORS

Apple Pie

Banana Bread

Orange Cranberry Cake

Carrot Cake

Sweet Corn Drops

Margarita

Curd Filled

Boston and Bavarian Cream

Huckleberry Cheesecake

Strawberry Shortcake

German Chocolate

Red Velvet

Chocolate Chocolate Chip

Candy-Filled Chocolate Drops

Cocoa Nib

Mocha

Hot Chocolate

S'mores

Chocolate Peanut Butter

Chocolate Hazelnut Filled

Chocolate Cream Filled

Chocolate Coconut Macaroon Doughnut Holes

Brandied Eggnog

Crème Brûlée

PB & J

Herb and Spice

Chai

Date and Walnut

Maple Bacon Bars

APPLE PIE

Part doughnut, part fried pie, these doughnuts are all apple-y goodness. Tart pie apples, such as Granny Smiths, make the best filling.

Makes 6 to 12 doughnuts

   1 cup cooking apples, cut into ¼-inch dice

   1 tablespoon freshly squeezed lemon juice

   2 tablespoons (25 grams) superfine sugar

   ¼ teaspoon ground allspice

   ¼ teaspoon cinnamon

   1 teaspoon vanilla extract

   2 teaspoons arrowroot

   1 batch Apple Cider dough (page 34) or Old-Fashioned Sour Cream dough (page 30)

   1 tablespoon milk or water

   Cinnamon Spice glaze (page 50) or Caramel glaze (page 51)

1. Combine the apples, lemon juice, and sugar in a heavy-bottomed pot over medium heat until the sugar is melted. Stir in the allspice, cinnamon, vanilla, and arrowroot. Simmer until the mixture thickens, about 2 minutes. Remove from heat and set aside.

2. Prepare the chosen dough as directed, but roll out the dough to just a bit less than ½ inch thick. Cut into 3-inch-diameter rounds. Roll out half of the rounds to about a 3¼-inch diameter. To assemble, lightly brush each wider round with the milk and place a tablespoon of the filling in the center of each. Spread evenly, leaving a ¼-inch margin around the edge. Top with a smaller rounds and lightly pinch to seal. Then recut with the same cutter, sealing the edges.

3. Fry as directed, allowing the doughnuts to cool slightly before glazing.

BANANA BREAD

Banana keeps these doughnuts moist, so they keep well for a day or two, but I can't resist them when they are still warm with a crisp crust.

Makes 6 to 12 doughnuts

1 batch Basic Cake dough (page 17), Vegan Cake dough (page 26), or Chocolate Cake dough (page 28), reducing the ½ cup milk to ⅓ cup

1 banana, mashed

Pinch of cardamom (optional)

¼ cup pecans, chopped (optional)

Maple glaze (page 48)

1. Prepare the chosen dough as directed. Mix in the banana, cardamom, and pecans after adding the wet ingredients until just combined; be sure not to overmix or your doughnuts may end up rubbery.

2. Pipe and fry as directed, allowing the doughnuts to cool slightly before glazing.

ORANGE CRANBERRY CAKE

The smell of these doughnuts always transports me to the holidays. They are the perfect accompaniment to a warm fire and a cup of tea.

Makes 6 to 12 doughnuts

> 1 batch Basic Cake dough (page 17), Gluten-Free Cake dough (page 23), or Vegan Cake dough (page 26)
>
> 1 teaspoon ground cinnamon
>
> 2 tablespoons dried cranberries
>
> 1 tablespoon orange zest
>
> ¼ cup pecans, finely chopped (optional)
>
> Citrus glaze (page 48)

1. Prepare the chosen dough as directed, replacing the nutmeg with the cinnamon. After adding the wet ingredients, mix in the cranberries, orange zest, and pecans.

2. Pipe and fry as directed, allowing the doughnuts to cool slightly before glazing.

CARROT CAKE

My friend Shauna makes the best carrot cake around. Her secret? Reduce the carrot juice to a syrup for intense carroty sweetness. Top these with a whipped cream cheese frosting or use a simple sugar glaze. *Photo on page 52.*

Makes 6 to 12 doughnuts

2 cups carrot juice

1 batch Basic Cake dough (page 17)

½ teaspoon ground cloves

1 ½ teaspoons ground ginger

1 ½ teaspoons ground cinnamon

½ cup finely grated carrot

¼ cup walnuts, finely chopped

¼ cup golden raisins

Cream Cheese Frosting (page 78)

¼ cup crushed pecans or shredded or flaked coconut (optional)

1. Bring the carrot juice to a boil over medium heat. Reduce the heat to low and simmer slowly, stirring occasionally, until reduced to about ½ cup of syrup, 20 to 30 minutes. Remove from the heat and let cool.

2. Prepare the dough as directed, replacing the nutmeg with the cloves, ginger, and cinnamon, and the milk with the carrot syrup. After adding the wet ingredients, fold in the carrots, walnuts, and raisins.

3. Pipe rings and fry as directed, allowing the doughnuts to cool slightly before frosting. Spread the cooled doughnuts with the frosting and garnish with pecans or coconut.

SWEET CORN DROPS

These cornbread-like doughnuts are best made in late summer when you can cut the corn off the cob yourself. But you can substitute frozen corn out of season as well.

Makes 25 to 30 drop doughnuts

>1 batch Basic Cake dough (page 17)
>
>¼ cup (40 grams) cornmeal
>
>¼ cup (75 grams) honey
>
>1 teaspoon freshly grated lemon zest
>
>¼ cup sweet corn
>
>Honey glaze (page 48) (optional)

1. Prepare the dough as directed, replacing ¼ cup of the all-purpose flour with cornmeal, the sugar with the honey, and the nutmeg with the lemon zest. After adding the wet ingredients, fold in the corn.

2. For rings, pipe and fry as directed.

3. To make rustic drop-style doughnuts, reduce the oil heat to 330°F. Drop rounded spoonfuls of the batter into the oil and cook to a light golden brown.

4. Let cool slightly before glazing, or serve them warm with honey butter.

MARGARITA

You're not likely to find tequila, lime, and salt topping the doughnuts in your local bakery. Good thing you can make them yourself! Fleur de Sel adds a distinctive flavor; if not available, use another good-quality sea salt. For an extra kick of lime, try filling these doughnuts with lime curd (using the Basic Fruit Curd recipe on page 64).

Makes 8 to 14 doughnuts

> 1 batch any Raised dough
>
> 1 teaspoon freshly grated lime zest
>
> ½ cup (50 grams) confectioners' sugar
>
> 2 teaspoons (about ½ lime) freshly squeezed lime juice
>
> 1 teaspoon tequila
>
> Fleur de Sel (optional)
>
> Lime zest for garnish (optional)

1. Prepare the chosen dough as directed, replacing the vanilla with the lime zest, and fry or bake as directed.

2. To make the glaze, sift the confectioners' sugar into a wide bowl, large enough to dip your doughnut rounds in. Stir in the lime juice and tequila until smooth. Dip each cooled doughnut into the glaze and set on a rack to dry. Sprinkle with Fleur de Sel and lime zest.

CURD FILLED

Fruit curds are more tangy than typical fruit preserves, and they make a much more luscious filling for doughnuts. Any leftover curd is amazing stirred into yogurt or spread onto toast.

Makes 6 to 12 doughnuts

> 1 batch Basic Fruit Curd (recipe follows)
>
> 1 batch Basic Raised dough (page 2) or Chocolate Raised dough (page 11)
>
> Basic Sugar glaze (page 47) or Citrus glaze (page 48)

1. Begin by preparing the fruit curd filling as directed. While the fruit curd is cooling, prepare the chosen dough for filled rounds and fry as directed.

2. When the doughnuts have cooled, fill a pastry bag fitted with a Bismarck (#230) tip with the fruit curd. Holding a doughnut in one hand, plunge the tip into the side of the doughnut, pushing it about ¾ inch deep. Gently squeeze the pastry bag to fill the doughnut, withdrawing the tip slowly as you squeeze; you will feel the doughnut expand slightly as you fill it. Repeat with the remaining doughnuts. Glaze the tops and let set before serving.

Basic Fruit Curd

> ½ cup (100 grams) superfine sugar
>
> 5 egg yolks, lightly beaten
>
> 1 batch curd flavor mixture (recipes follow)
>
> ¼ cup (½ stick) butter

1. In the top of a double boiler or a non-reactive saucepan, whisk the sugar and egg yolks. Stir in the curd flavor mixture and heat over simmering water (or low heat if not using a double boiler), stirring constantly, until the mixture thickens slightly and reaches 160°F, 10 to 15 minutes. Remove

the pan from the heat and stir in the butter, 1 tablespoon at a time, incorporating each completely before adding the next. Allow the mixture to cool to room temperature, cover, and refrigerate for up to 2 weeks.

Citrus Curd

¼ cup freshly squeezed citrus juice

2 tablespoons freshly grated citrus zest

1. Combine the citrus juice and zest.

Berry Curd

2 pints fresh berries

1 tablespoon freshly grated lemon zest

1. Heat the berries in a medium saucepan over medium heat just until they start to soften, then push through a strainer. Combine ¼ cup of the berry juice with the lemon zest, reserving the rest of the juice for another use.

Stone Fruit Curd

2 cups sliced juicy stone fruit (apricots, plums, peaches)

Juice of 1 lemon

1. Heat the fruit in a medium saucepan over medium heat until the slices fall apart. Transfer to a blender and blend until smooth. Combine ½ cup of the purée with the lemon juice, reserving the rest of the purée for another use.

BOSTON AND BAVARIAN CREAM

Rich, eggy pastry cream is the key to a perfect Boston or Bavarian Cream doughnut; the only difference is the glaze, so it's easy to make a half-and-half batch.

Makes 6 to 12 doughnuts

1 cup whole milk

1 vanilla bean, split lengthwise

Pinch of salt

¼ cup (60 grams) superfine sugar

1 tablespoon cornstarch

1 large egg

1 tablespoon butter

1 batch Basic Raised dough (page 2) or Gluten-Free Basic Raised dough (page 7)

Chocolate glaze (page 47)

Confectioners' sugar

1. Start by making the pastry cream. Set a fine sieve over a medium bowl and set aside.

2. Combine the milk, vanilla bean, and salt in a heavy-bottomed pan over medium heat. Bring just to a boil, stirring constantly.

3. In a small bowl, whisk together the sugar and cornstarch. Beat in the egg. Warm the egg mixture by slowly drizzling in one-third of the hot milk, whisking constantly. Add the warmed egg mixture to the pot with the remaining hot milk. Continue to whisk, over medium heat, for about 2 minutes or until the mixture thickens. Immediately remove from the heat and pour the pastry cream through the sieve. Let the mixture cool for about 5 minutes, stirring occasionally to prevent a skin from forming.

4. When the cream has cooled slightly, add the butter and stir until blended.

5. Cover the bowl with plastic wrap pressed directly onto the cream's surface to prevent a skin from forming or any condensation from dripping onto the cream. Chill for at least 1 hour and up to 2 days. If the mixture separates, just whisk briskly until creamy.

6. Prepare the chosen dough for filled rounds and fry as directed.

7. When the doughnuts have cooled to the touch, spoon the pastry cream into a pastry bag fitted with a Bismarck (#230) tip. Holding a doughnut in one hand, plunge the tip into the side of the doughnut, pushing it about ¾ inch deep. Gently squeeze the pastry bag to fill the doughnut, withdrawing the tip slowly as you squeeze; you will feel the doughnut expand slightly as you fill it. Repeat with the remaining doughnuts.

8. For Boston Cream doughnuts, glaze the tops with the chocolate glaze and allow to set before serving. For Bavarian Cream doughnuts, dust each cooled, filled doughnut with confectioners' sugar.

HUCKLEBERRY CHEESECAKE

Blue mountain huckleberries were in season when I was experimenting with cheesecake-filled doughnuts, so they were an easy choice among the many fruits that would be delicious with this creamy filling. If huckleberries aren't available, try cherries, raspberries, strawberries, blueberries, or one of the fruit curds from the recipe on page 64.

Makes 6 to 12 doughnuts

> 1 batch Basic Raised dough (page 2) or Chocolate Raised dough (page 11)
>
> 2 ounces cream cheese, softened
>
> 2 tablespoons sweetened condensed milk
>
> 1 tablespoon plus 1 teaspoon freshly squeezed lemon juice, divided
>
> 1 tablespoon sour cream or plain yogurt
>
> ½ cup fresh huckleberries
>
> 1 tablespoon milk or water
>
> 1 tablespoon (37 grams) superfine sugar
>
> Graham Cracker Topping (recipe follows) (optional)

1. Prepare the chosen dough as directed to the proofing stage. While the dough proofs, prepare the filling.

2. In a small bowl, beat the cream cheese using a hand mixer until fluffy. Stir in the condensed milk, 1 tablespoon lemon juice, and sour cream. Beat until smooth. Chill for at least 1 hour before filling the doughnuts.

3. Combine the huckleberries, sugar, and remaining lemon juice in a heavy-bottomed pot over medium heat and stir until the huckleberries release some of their juices and the sugar has dissolved, about 5 minutes. Set aside.

4. When the dough has proofed, roll out on a lightly floured surface to just a bit more than ¼ inch thick. Cut into 3-inch-diameter rounds. Roll out half of the rounds to about a 3¼-inch diameter. To assemble, lightly brush each

wider round with the milk and place a heaping teaspoon of the cream cheese filling in the center of each large round, topped with a scant teaspoon of fruit filling. Top with the smaller rounds and lightly pinch to seal. Then recut with the same cutter, sealing the edges.

5. Let the doughnuts proof for 5 to 20 minutes in a warm room, then fry as directed. Dip the top of each doughnut in the graham cracker mixture while still warm.

Graham Cracker Topping

½ cup graham cracker crumbs

1 tablespoon (12 grams) superfine sugar

2 tablespoons butter, melted

1. In a small bowl, mix together the graham cracker crumbs, sugar, and butter.

STRAWBERRY SHORTCAKE

The Donut Man shop in Glendora, California, may not look like much from outside. Inside, however, if the season is right, you'll find out why folks flock there: strawberry shortcake doughnuts, piled high with farm-fresh fruit. This version is a little easier to assemble, but just as tasty. At the height of summer, take another hint from Donut Man and substitute juicy slices of fresh peaches.

Makes 6 to 12 doughnuts

> 1 batch Ricotta dough (page 33) or any Cake dough
>
> 1 cup heavy cream
>
> 2 tablespoons confectioners' sugar, sifted, plus additional for dusting (optional)
>
> 1 teaspoon vanilla
>
> 1 pint fresh strawberries, washed, hulled, and sliced

1. Prepare the chosen dough and fry or bake as directed for rings.

2. While the doughnuts are cooling, whip the heavy cream, sugar, and vanilla until soft peaks form.

3. Top each doughnut with a dollop of whipped cream and 2 or 3 tablespoons of strawberries, or cut doughnuts in half and sandwich whipped cream and strawberries between. Dust lightly with confectioners' sugar.

GERMAN CHOCOLATE

When I was a child my favorite cake was German Chocolate. I couldn't resist running a finger (or five) through the bowl of rich, nutty frosting before the cake was sliced. But these doughnuts are so heavenly, you'll want to devote every bit of frosting to the intended destination.

Makes 6 to 12 doughnuts

> 1 batch Chocolate Cake dough (page 28)
>
> ½ cup evaporated milk
>
> ½ cup (120 grams) superfine sugar
>
> 1 egg yolk, beaten with 1 teaspoon water
>
> ¼ cup (½ stick) butter
>
> ½ cup chopped pecans
>
> ½ cup flaked coconut
>
> 1 teaspoon vanilla extract

1. Prepare the doughnuts as directed and let cool.

2. Combine the evaporated milk, sugar, egg yolk, and butter in a heavy-bottomed pot over medium heat and stir until thick, about 12 minutes. Remove from the heat and stir in the pecans, coconut, and vanilla. Continue to stir until the frosting cools, then spread about 1 tablespoon on top of each doughnut.

RED VELVET

Red velvet cake makes a dramatic presentation, and these doughnuts—with their deep red, subtly chocolate cake and whipped cream cheese frosting—are equally impressive.

Makes 6 to 12 doughnuts

> 1 batch Basic Cake dough (page 17), Baked Cake dough (page 21), or Gluten-Free Cake dough (page 23)
>
> ¼ cup (27 grams) Dutch processed cocoa powder
>
> ¼ cup (60 grams) superfine sugar
>
> 2 teaspoons red food coloring
>
> 2 teaspoons white vinegar
>
> Cream Cheese Frosting (recipe follows)
>
> ¼ cup crushed pecans or shredded or flaked coconut (optional)

1. Prepare the chosen dough as directed, but omit the nutmeg and stir in the cocoa powder and additional ¼ cup sugar along with the dry ingredients. Add the red food coloring and vinegar to the wet ingredients and proceed as directed.

2. Spread the cooled doughnuts with the frosting and garnish with pecans or coconut.

Cream Cheese Frosting

> 4 ounces cream cheese, softened
>
> 1 cup confectioners' sugar, sifted
>
> ¼ cup (½ stick or 2 ounces) unsalted butter, softened
>
> ½ teaspoon vanilla extract

1. In the bowl of a stand mixer fitted with the paddle attachment, whip the cream cheese, sugar, butter, and vanilla on low speed until creamy. Increase the speed to high and mix until light and fluffy, about 5 minutes, scraping down the sides of the bowl as needed. Cover and refrigerate for at least 1 hour before using.

Variation: Whisk in 1 tablespoon strained raspberry or other fruit jam, or even a little bit of food coloring, along with the vanilla.

CHOCOLATE CHOCOLATE CHIP

Chocolate chip doughnuts are delicious . . . but *chocolate* chocolate chip doughnuts are a chocolate lover's dream come true.

Makes 6 to 12 doughnuts

> 1 batch Chocolate Cake dough (page 28)
>
> 1/3 cup chocolate chips
>
> Basic Sugar glaze (page 47)

1. Prepare the dough as directed; after adding the wet ingredients, mix in the chocolate chips.

2. Roll and fry the doughnuts as directed, allowing them to cool slightly before glazing.

CANDY-FILLED CHOCOLATE DROPS

I spied this fun trick in a *Martha Stewart Everyday Food* magazine—little bite-size doughnut holes stuffed with caramel candy. As the doughnuts cook, the candy melts into a perfect oozy center. Caramel is a great option, but I say try your favorite candies: Reese's Peanut Butter Cups, Hershey's Kisses, Snickers, you name it.

Makes 15 to 20 doughnuts

> 1 batch Chocolate Cake dough (page 28)
>
> Your favorite meltable candy, cut into 15 to 20 half-inch pieces
>
> Basic Sugar glaze (page 47) (optional)
>
> Confectioners' sugar or cocoa powder (optional)

1. Prepare the dough as directed, rolling to about ¼ inch thick. Cut out 1-by-2-inch rectangles. Place a candy chunk about ½ inch in from one edge and fold the top over to enclose the candy. Press lightly to seal, then fry as directed.

2. Glaze or dust with confectioners' sugar or cocoa powder.

COCOA NIB

Cocoa nibs add a subtle nutty taste and unexpected crunch to simple cake doughnuts. They work equally well with plain cake or chocolate cake dough.

Makes 6 to 12 doughnuts

> 1 batch any Cake dough
>
> ¼ cup cocoa nibs
>
> Basic Sugar glaze (page 47)

1. Prepare the chosen dough as directed; after adding the wet ingredients, mix in the cocoa nibs.

2. Roll or pipe and fry or bake the doughnuts as directed, allowing the doughnuts to cool slightly before glazing.

MOCHA

Coffee and doughnuts come together in this decadent morning or evening treat.

Makes 6 to 12 doughnuts

> 1 batch Chocolate Cake dough (page 28)
>
> 2 tablespoons brewed espresso, divided
>
> Chocolate glaze (page 47)

1. Prepare the dough as directed, replacing the vanilla with 1½ tablespoons of the espresso.

2. Roll and fry the doughnuts as directed, allowing them to cool slightly before glazing.

3. Make the chocolate glaze as directed, replacing the vanilla with the remaining espresso.

HOT CHOCOLATE

Kick your chocolate doughnuts up a notch with a bit of spice. A little cinnamon and cayenne pepper transform the ordinary chocolate cake doughnut into something special. For an added kick, mix a pinch of cayenne pepper into the glaze.

Makes 6 to 12 doughnuts

> 1 batch Chocolate Cake dough (page 28)
>
> ½ teaspoon cayenne pepper
>
> 1 teaspoon cinnamon
>
> Basic Sugar glaze (page 47) or Chocolate glaze (page 47)

1. Prepare the dough as directed, adding the cayenne pepper and cinnamon to the dry ingredients.

2. Roll and fry the doughnuts as directed, allowing them to cool slightly before glazing.

S'MORES

Like s'mores around the campfire, these treats need to be eaten immediately while the chocolate and marshmallow are still ooey-gooey. If you want a similar doughnut that you can take with you to a party, fill with marshmallow crème, then glaze with chocolate. The glaze really is optional, for when you want an intensely sweet hit; these doughnut s'mores are sweet without it.

Makes 6 to 12 doughnuts

> 4 tablespoons unsalted butter, melted, divided
>
> 10 graham crackers, finely crushed
>
> 2 teaspoons (10 grams) superfine sugar
>
> 1 batch Basic Raised dough (page 2) or Chocolate Raised dough (page 11)
>
> 1 tablespoon milk or water
>
> Twelve 1-ounce squares milk or dark chocolate
>
> 48 mini marshmallows
>
> Basic Sugar glaze (page 47) or Chocolate glaze (page 47) (optional)

1. Stir together 3 tablespoons of the melted butter, graham crackers, and sugar. Cover and set aside.

2. Prepare the chosen dough as directed through the proofing stage. Roll the dough to just a bit more than ¼ inch thick. Cut into 3-inch-diameter rounds. Roll out half of the rounds to about a 3¼-inch diameter. To assemble, lightly brush each wider round with the milk and place a square of chocolate and 4 mini marshmallows in the center of each. Top with the smaller rounds and lightly pinch to seal. Then recut with the same cutter, sealing the edges.

3. Fry the doughnuts as directed and let cool for only 3 minutes. Glaze or brush each doughnut with a little melted butter, then dip into the graham cracker mixture. Serve immediately.

CHOCOLATE PEANUT BUTTER

Get your chocolate in your peanut butter with this doughnut version of a Reese's Peanut Butter Cup.

Makes 6 to 12 doughnuts

> 1 batch Chocolate Raised dough (page 11)
>
> 1 cup creamy peanut butter
>
> 3 tablespoons unsalted butter
>
> ⅔ cup (66 grams) confectioners' sugar
>
> Chocolate glaze (page 47) or Basic Sugar glaze (page 47)

1. Prepare the dough for filled rounds and fry as directed.

2. In a medium bowl, whip together the peanut butter and butter using a hand mixer until creamy. Sift in the sugar and beat until light and fluffy, about 2 minutes. Spoon the peanut butter filling into a pastry bag fitted with a Bismarck (#230) tip. Fill the doughnuts as directed in step 7 on page 68.

3. Glaze the tops and let set before serving.

CHOCOLATE HAZELNUT FILLED

Chocolate hazelnut spreads like Nutella or Loacker make an addictively delicious filling for raised doughnuts. Adding a little whipped cream lightens the spread a bit, making it a little less rich and a little easier to pipe into the doughnuts.

Makes 6 to 12 doughnuts

> 1 batch Basic Raised dough (page 2)
>
> 1 cup chocolate hazelnut spread
>
> ½ cup heavy cream
>
> Chocolate glaze (page 47) or Basic Sugar glaze (page 47)

1. Prepare the dough for filled rounds and fry as directed.

2. In a medium bowl, whip together the chocolate spread and cream using a hand mixer until smooth and fluffy. Spoon the filling into a pastry bag fitted with a Bismarck (#230) tip and fill the doughnuts as directed in step 7 on page 68.

3. Glaze the tops and let set before serving.

CHOCOLATE CREAM FILLED

These chocolate cream–filled doughnuts are inspired by my childhood favorites from Dunkin' Donuts, in which the chocolate filling is more whipped cream than ganache. If you like your chocolate filling a bit richer, up the cocoa powder to 3 tablespoons.

Makes 6 to 12 doughnuts

> 1 batch Basic Raised dough (page 2), Gluten-Free Basic Raised dough (page 7), or Chocolate Raised dough (page 11)
>
> 1 cup heavy cream
>
> ½ teaspoon vanilla extract
>
> 1 tablespoon (15 grams) superfine sugar
>
> 1 ½ tablespoons Dutch processed cocoa powder
>
> Confectioners' sugar

1. Prepare the chosen dough for filled rounds and fry as directed.

2. Prepare the filling by lightly mixing together the whipping cream, vanilla, sugar, and cocoa powder. Cover and refrigerate for 15 minutes. Whip the mixture to soft peaks.

3. Spoon the whipped filling into a pastry bag fitted with a ¼-inch star tip and fill the doughnuts as directed in step 7 on page 68.

4. Roll the cooled doughnuts in confectioners' sugar and serve.

CHOCOLATE COCONUT MACAROON DOUGHNUT HOLES

These little coconut treats are quite rich, so I like to just make bite-size holes rather than full rings. Stored in an airtight container, they are just as good the next day.

Makes 15 to 20 doughnut holes

> 1 batch Chocolate Cake dough (page 28)
>
> 3 egg whites
>
> Pinch of cream of tartar
>
> 6 tablespoons (90 grams) superfine sugar
>
> 1 ½ cups shredded coconut, divided

1. Prepare the dough as directed and cut out doughnut holes. Fry as directed and allow the doughnut holes to cool slightly.

2. Preheat the oven to 400°F.

3. Beat the egg whites with the cream of tartar until stiff. Gradually beat in the sugar until the meringue becomes smooth and glossy. Fold in ½ cup of the coconut.

4. Place the remaining coconut in a bowl and line a baking sheet with parchment. Dip most of each doughnut hole in the meringue, roll in the coconut, and place on the baking sheet. Bake until the tops just start to brown, about 5 minutes. Cool on a rack before serving.

BRANDIED EGGNOG

Make the holiday season just a little more so with these festive doughnuts. Sprinkling the tops with nutmeg not only adds a spicy zing but also gives them a tantalizing eggnog appearance.

Makes 6 to 12 doughnuts

> 1 batch Old-Fashioned Sour Cream dough (page 30), Basic Cake dough (page 17), or Baked Cake dough (page 21)
>
> ½ cup eggnog
>
> 2 tablespoons brandy, divided
>
> Brown Butter glaze (page 50)
>
> Freshly grated nutmeg (optional)

1. Prepare the chosen dough as directed, reducing the sugar to 3 tablespoons and replacing the milk with eggnog and the vanilla with 1 tablespoon brandy. Fry or bake as directed.

2. To make the glaze, prepare as directed, replacing the milk with the remaining brandy.

3. After the doughnuts have cooled slightly, glaze them and serve. Dust the tops with freshly grated nutmeg.

CRÈME BRÛLÉE

Fluffy pastry, creamy goodness, and a perfect caramel crackle: these doughnuts bring a new level of sophistication to a favorite treat.

Makes 6 to 12 doughnuts

½ cup whole milk

½ cup heavy cream

½ vanilla bean, split lengthwise

¾ cup (180 grams) superfine sugar, divided

2 egg yolks

1 batch Basic Raised dough (page 2), Gluten-Free Basic Raised dough (page 7), or Chocolate Raised dough (page 11)

1. In a medium saucepan set over medium heat, bring the milk, cream, and vanilla bean to a simmer. Meanwhile, whisk together ¼ cup of the sugar and the egg yolks in a large bowl until the mixture is pale. When the milk mixture is hot, slowly pour it over the egg yolk mixture, whisking constantly to prevent the eggs from curdling. Return the mixture to the saucepan and continue cooking until the mixture thickens, 2 to 3 minutes. Remove from the heat and continue whisking until smooth. Pour the custard into a bowl and cover with plastic wrap, pressing it directly onto the surface of the custard. Chill for at least 2 hours.

2. Prepare the chosen dough for filled rounds and fry as directed.

3. Fill a pastry bag fitted with a Bismarck (#230) tip with the custard and fill the doughnuts as directed in step 7 on page 68.

4. Dip the doughnut tops in the remaining sugar to thickly coat, then place sugar side up on a baking sheet. Sprinkle a little more sugar on top if needed. Use a kitchen torch to slowly caramelize the sugar until golden. Alternatively, use the broiler on high. Let cool so the sugar hardens.

PB & J

These PB & J doughnuts are seriously and deliciously messy. Eat them almost immediately or the doughnut will get soggy.

Makes 6 to 12 doughnuts

> 1 batch Basic Raised dough (page 2) or Gluten-Free Basic Raised dough (page 7)
>
> ½ cup creamy peanut butter
>
> 2 tablespoons confectioners' sugar
>
> 2 tablespoons heavy cream
>
> ¼ cup raspberry jam
>
> Honey glaze (page 48)

1. Prepare the chosen dough for filled rounds and fry as directed.

2. In a medium bowl, beat the peanut butter, sugar, and cream until smooth and light. Chill for about 15 minutes.

3. Spoon the peanut butter cream into a pastry bag fitted with a Bismarck (#230) tip and fill the doughnuts as directed in step 7 on page 68.

4. Spoon the jam into another pastry bag fitted with the same size Bismarck tip. Fill doughnuts through the same hole, angling the tip up slightly, being careful not to puncture the surface of the doughnut.

5. Glaze the tops and allow to set before serving.

HERB AND SPICE

Take simple cake doughnuts from ordinary to intriguing with just a hint of herbs and spices. Lavender pairs beautifully with vanilla, as long as you are careful and don't overdo it. Fennel seeds don't usually find their way into sweets, but an artful blending with orange brings out their nutty side. Browse your spice drawer and see what other combinations you can try.

Makes 6 to 12 doughnuts

> 1 batch Old-Fashioned Sour Cream dough (page 30) or any Cake dough
>
> Spice mixture (recipes follow)
>
> Basic Sugar glaze (page 47)

1. Prepare the chosen dough as directed, omitting the nutmeg. After adding the wet ingredients, fold in the spice mixture. Fry or bake as directed, allowing the doughnuts to cool slightly before glazing.

Rosemary and Honey

> 1 teaspoon finely chopped fresh rosemary
>
> 1 tablespoon honey

Lavender and Vanilla

> 1 teaspoon finely chopped culinary lavender
>
> 1 tablespoon vanilla extract

Fennel and Orange

> 1 teaspoon fennel seeds, toasted and crushed
>
> 1 tablespoon freshly grated orange zest

Poppy Seed and Lemon

> 1 tablespoon poppy seeds
>
> 2 tablespoons freshly grated lemon zest

CHAI

I still recall the sweet, spicy warmth of my first cup of chai. By infusing the milk with black tea, you create a true chai flavor in every bite.

Makes 6 to 12 doughnuts

⅔ cup whole milk

2 tablespoons black tea leaves

½ teaspoon ground ginger

½ teaspoon ground cinnamon

½ teaspoon freshly ground cardamom

½ teaspoon freshly grated nutmeg

¼ teaspoon freshly ground black pepper

1 batch Basic Cake dough (page 17) or Chocolate Cake dough (page 28)

Basic Sugar glaze (page 47)

1. Scald the milk in a medium pot and add the tea leaves. Steep for about 5 minutes, then strain.

2. In a small bowl, mix together the ginger, cinnamon, cardamom, nutmeg, and pepper.

3. Prepare the chosen dough as directed, replacing the nutmeg with the spice mix and the plain milk with ⅓ cup of the tea-infused milk. Reserve the remaining tea-infused milk for the glaze. Fry the doughnuts as directed.

4. To make the glaze, prepare as directed, replacing the plain milk with the reserved tea-infused milk, adding a pinch of cardamom if desired.

5. After the doughnuts have cooled slightly, glaze them and serve.

DATE AND WALNUT

Inspired by a dense, dark tea cake, these doughnuts combine the same sticky sweet dates and nutty walnut crunch, but in a lighter pastry. Toasting the walnuts lightly gets rid of any bitterness.

Makes 6 to 12 doughnuts

> 1 batch Apple Cider dough (page 34) or any Cake dough
>
> ¼ cup Medjool dates, finely chopped
>
> ¼ cup lightly toasted walnuts, finely chopped
>
> Maple glaze (page 48)

1. Prepare the chosen dough as directed. After adding the wet ingredients, fold in the dates and walnuts.

2. Fry or bake as directed, allowing the doughnuts to cool slightly before glazing.

MAPLE BACON BARS

The salty sweetness of these bars are like the perfect pancake and bacon breakfast. If you want even more bacon flavor, try replacing the shortening in the dough with bacon grease. Don't eat bacon? Try these bars with a sprinkle of flaked smoked salt instead.

Makes 8 to 14 doughnuts

> 1 batch Basic Raised dough (page 2) or Gluten-Free Basic Raised dough (page 7)
>
> 6 strips bacon
>
> Maple glaze (page 48)

1. Prepare the chosen dough as directed, cutting into 2-by-4-inch rectangles instead of rings. Fry as directed and let cool slightly.

2. Fry the bacon until crisp and cut each strip in half crosswise.

3. Dip each bar into the maple glaze, then top with a piece of bacon. Let the glaze set before serving.

DOUGHNUT-MAKING RESOURCES AND SUPPLIES

You can find specialty doughnut-making equipment at most kitchen supply stores. Here are a few additional suggestions to help you along:

Bob's Red Mill Natural Foods
www.bobsredmill.com
Specialty flours (including gluten-free)

Crate & Barrel
www.crateandbarrel.com
Thermometers, pastry cloth

King Arthur Flour
www.kingarthurflour.com
Specialty flours (including gluten-free), doughnut cutters, pans, makers, mixes, glazing sugar, pastry cloth

Sur La Table
www.surlatable.com
Doughnut cutters, pastry bags, pastry cloths, pastry tips, thermometers, deep fryer

Target
www.target.com
Doughnut pans, doughnut droppers, deep fryers

Thermoworks
www.thermoworks.com
Thermapen thermometers

Williams-Sonoma
www.williams-sonoma.com
Pastry bags with filling tips, deep fryers, thermometers, pastry cloth, doughnut cutters

INDEX

Note: Page numbers in italic refer to photographs.

ACKNOWLEDGMENTS

An enormous thank-you to the wonderful team at Sasquatch Books. From your initial excitement about this project and faith in me throughout the book's development, you've been a pillar of support in just the right way.

I was inspired and educated by a wide variety of sources, but there are a couple of noteworthy ones that taught me how to make doughnuts in the first place. The first successful cake doughnuts I made were from a recipe on JoePastry.com—a site that features recipes and tips that really work. I have not found a better source for learning pastry techniques than Bo Friberg's *The Professional Pastry Chef*, and without it I might never have arrived at my raised dough recipes.

A special thank-you to Shauna and Danny Ahern for their wonderful insights into gluten-free baking. Yes, you can make doughnuts gluten free!

A huge thanks to my recipes testers: Bria Mertens, Caitlin Pierce, Carolyn Cope, Carolyn Pickton, Clair Sutton, Deeba Rajpal, Aparna Balasubramanian, Elizabeth Nyland, Helen McSweeney, Jamie Schler, Jennifer Eggleston, Jill Lightner, Linda Nguyen, Susan Roxborough, Anda, Lucy Vaserfirer, Andrew Vaserfirer, Maggie McConnell, Melinda Knapp, Cindy Ensley, M. Lynn Yu, Sheena Starky, Jess Thomson, Tom Bauer, Danielle Tsi, Tara Barker, and Tara O'Brady. Your great comments and questions made both the book and the doughnuts better!

I owe both Matt Wright and David Silver a debt and some doughnuts for graciously lending me their cameras after mine died midway through the photo shoot.

Finally, I never would have attempted to write this book without the encouragement, gentle nudging, and honest feedback from my wonderful husband, Cameron. You said I should do it and you were right.

ABOUT THE AUTHOR

Lara Ferroni is a tech geek turned food geek who spends her days exploring the food culture of the Pacific Northwest. As a writer and photographer, you might spy her learning to make kimchi in the back room of a local church, foraging for wild berries, or snapping away in some of Seattle's finest kitchens. You can find her work in publications such as *Seattle* magazine, *Seattle Metropolitan*, Edible Communities, Epicurious.com, as well as in numerous cookbooks. You can find more of her tasty photos and recipes on her blog, www.cookandeat.com.